COLORING BOOK

MARTY NOBL

D1473555

DOVER PUBLICATIONS, INC.
Mineola, New York

NOTE

Day of the Dead is a Mexican holiday celebrated throughout the world. It is dedicated to the remembrance of deceased family and friends. It is held on November 1st and 2nd to coincide with the Roman Catholic holidays of All Saints' Day and All Souls' Day. Many scholars believe the origin of Day of the Dead celebrations can be traced back to an Aztec festival in honor of the goddess Mictecacihuatl. In Aztec mythology she was the Queen of the Underworld and guarded the bones of the dead. In indigenous art Mictecaichuatl was always represented as a fleshless skeleton and this image has inspired the thirty-one dazzling designs in this book. Created by noted artist Marty Noble, here is an amazing variety of skulls and skeletons waiting for a creative colorist to bring them to life.

Bibliographical Note

Day of the Dead Coloring Book is a new work, first published by Dover Publications, Inc., in 2013.

International Standard Book Number
ISBN-13: 978-0-486-49213-1
ISBN-10: 0-486-49213-3

Manufactured in the United States by Courier Corporation
49213305   2015
www.doverpublications.com

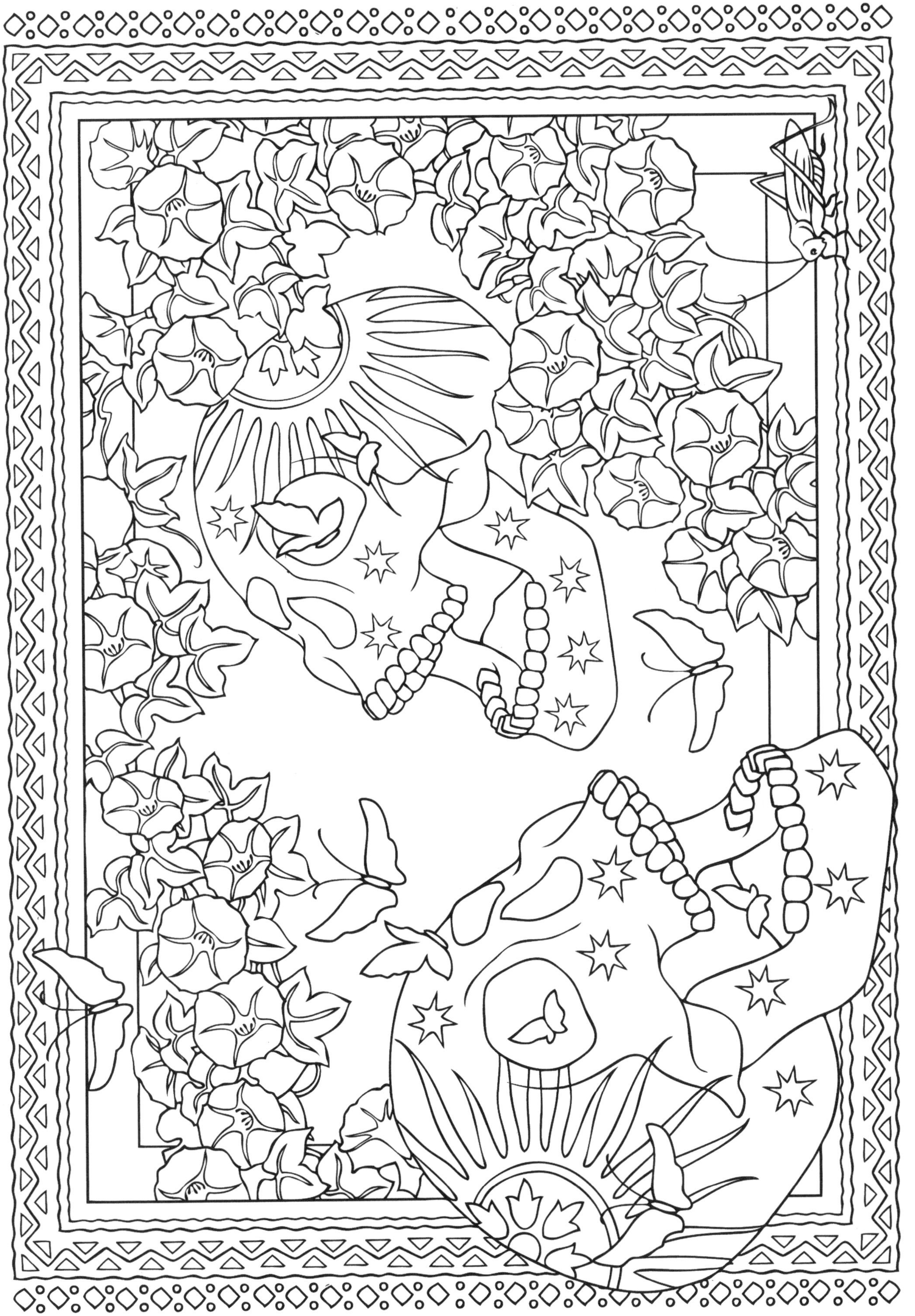

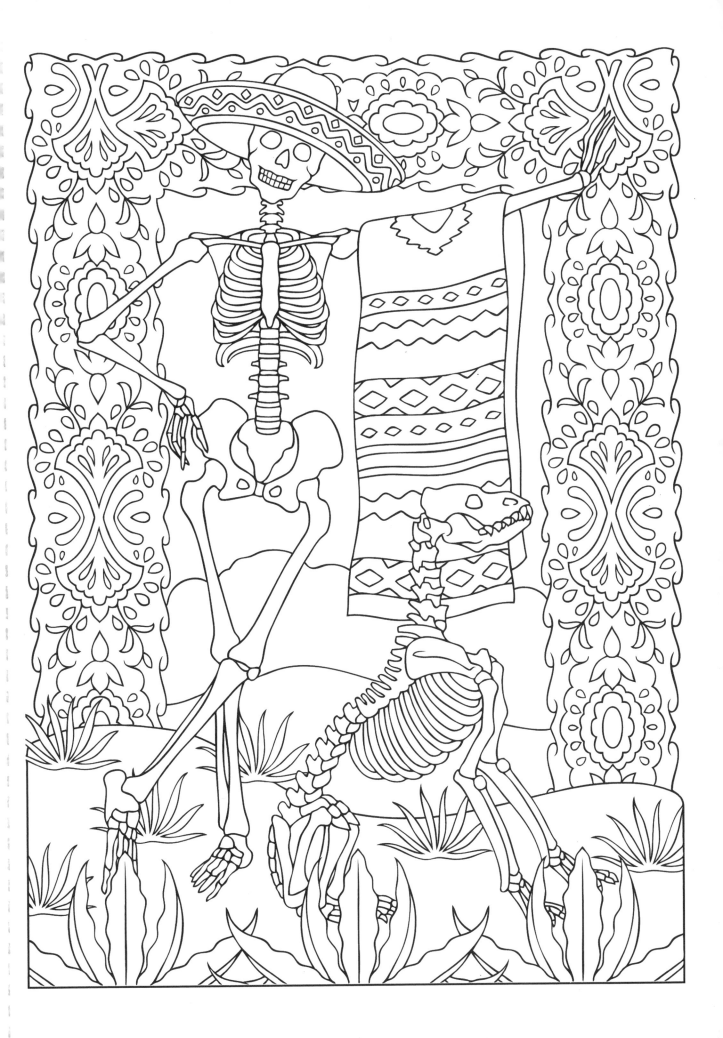